A book of poetry

Human Resources
by Rachel Zolf

Published by

Coach House Books
Toronto

Credits

  Canada

Published with the assistance of the Canada Council for the Arts and the Ontario Arts Council. The publisher also acknowledges the financial support of the Government of Ontario through the Ontario Book Publishing Tax Credit Program and the Government of Canada through the Book Publishing Industry Development Program.

Cataloguing information

LIBRARY AND ARCHIVES CANADA

CATALOGUING IN PUBLICATION

Zolf, Rachel
    Human resources / Rachel Zolf. -- 1st ed.

Poems.
ISBN 978-1-55245-182-3

    I. Title.

PS8599.O627H84 2007   C811'.54   C2007-900948-4

An epigraph

Because literature concerns itself with the ambiguities of the human condition, it stands as a threat to the vitality of the business executive, who must at all times maintain a bias towards action ... It is far safer to stick with throwaway thrillers, which at least provide a distraction from the stresses of the day. Forget the deep stuff. Read anything by Tom Clancy, Robert Ludlum or Jeffrey Archer ... And while you're at it, read the *Harvard Business Review*.

– editorial, *Harvard Business Review*

Start here The job is to write in 'plain language.' No adjectives, adornment or surfeit of meaning nuclear increasing[w1269]. All excess excised save the discrete pithy moment. Sonnet's rising eight lines, sublime orgasmic turn, dying six: perfect expenditure. Brisk stride along the green green grounds, sudden dip, ha-ha!

New performance weightings a bit of a moving target the future liability of make this sing.

Just to make sure we're speaking the same language we no longer have to use this caveat existing amounts grandfathered.

We'll have to wrap our heads around clear as mud I would like to move the goal posts.

Chunk it down into various links I'm totally medicated as I type.

Given enough input elements, a writing machine can spew about anything: private jets, exquisite gardens, offshore-banking havens, the Great Ephemeral Skin, how much we love our passionate$^{(Q8992)}$ francesca snazzy prat employees, how you breathe life into our Mission, Vision, Values, what we give you if you lose one finger$^{(Q691)}$ fool dance then gold on one hand and three toes on one foot (25% of the premiums you've paid for years), or three fingers on one hand and four toes (50%) or two hands and two feet (75%!). Unlike poetry, it flows with ease and on the same page as BMO banker Barrett: 'a student who can divine$^{(Q2855)}$ pablo from swiss prostate patterns of imagery in Chaucer's *Canterbury Tales* can surely be taught the principles of double-entry accounting

I don't want to trip over this in the future from where I'm sitting can you suggest massages.

This will give you a sense of the 'new look' it seems the tail's wagging the tail this block of content has been rationalized.

We took this offline to firm up the 'one-stop shopping spot' for HR content requires minor refreshing.

My head's spinning in reverse 360s just to close the loop with you.

Valéry's poem was a machine for reproducing emotion. It spilled into surplus and shut down at age 20 for 20 years. Our poem starts up at 20, engorged with the Swan's brute blood, Leda's terrified vague fingers. Pen drips with piss, shit and violation, sometimes forgetting to breathe. The communicator is a mirror not creator of society and nine months after the first book, there may be a disconnect. Stride the white and sorrow black field open-sown on the radar screen, the Form Worship Maxim ringing

We're in a bit of a holding pattern right now providing you with a pulse on 'inquiring minds' I'd kill this sentence entirely.

On our side of the family my day got totally blown out of the water push back if you think this is a 'must have.'

We make the call a non-event communication accompaniment I can suggest hoarding words like gold.

The new 'go forward' content tailored especially to I'd wager a guess.

How to warm up your mental motor and find your Big Idea

Ask yourself:

- What is my prospect's problem?
- What pain does the prospect want to avoid?
- What is the Unique Selling Promise (USP) of this product?
- What do I need to say to keep the prospect reading?

Money pimps between man's need and next month's rent. Couldn't bear the anxiety, couldn't write$^{(G-5)}$ it's not just another mountain how much longer will you resist. Now we even have benefits, clean teeth regularly, may be eligible for a BONUS. Turn schizoanalytical about reaching the place where *more* channels discharge into wan frisbee of fishy $^{(Q5244)}$investment. Wonder if this fixation has any correlation with constipation, how vulnerable it feels to shit, like orgasm

On our side of the family, sweet bald-headed Jesus saw God write about being Jewish.

Not 'special treatment' but a sense of the 'new look' of nothing.

I took it offline to rebalance the cleansing act, how shiny her toothy smile.

Funny how the confined structure of snappy business attire means logorrheic ease.

If you spend six months writing policies for a corpora-
tion swallowing another and merging employees. And
you're forced to wear blue shirts and grey slacks to meet-
ings where white, middle-aged HR women bicker over
whether capri$^{(W25031)}$ odyssey polypeptide pants are
acceptable, how to spell 'beachwear' and how best to
deal with 'militant' employees asking to work less over-
time. Between meetings, one may be inflicted with little
choice but to look away while they laud Barbados as a
much less 'uppity'$^{(G-23)}$ he is a Black and terrible God
vacation spot than Jamaica. Oops that's a lie, there was
one worthwhile moment that will also be covered off in
a larger initiative re: language. Sometime near the end
of our tenure, the HR ladies learned that the acronym
for their new employee performance$^{(Q5116)}$ mold dias-
pora program translated as 'blow job' in French

lesbian, writeing [sic] you is like
loseing [sic] the shit, only worse.
While Jew voids the money, I
write over a narrow Jew.
Because these excesss [sic] acquire
as if money were a Jew for
acquireing [sic], you should write
your lesbian, while shit
acquires.

Early in the new millennium[G18] hello[Q18] of vagina america bitch cat, on our 35th birthday in fact, the *New York Times Magazine* declared that theory was dead – just when you'd gotten around to reading it. Here you go again, we're always 20 years behind the times, should've been checking out *écriture* chicks at the Montreal feminist book fair instead of popping bennies and caterwauling through *Romeo and Juliet* in high school. With close friends a generation[W2065] plenty ill older, you envy a certain ease with bodies, ideas (however dispersed). Change[G46] a wooden dragon a world as cold as stone accidentally on purpose management is accompanied by good communication avoiding drunk men at yet another poetry reading. Maybe if you'd come to writing through sex (or the other way 'round), she wouldn't feel so blocked about libidinal faro dnj[W54051] urng sitcoms economies, tackling *Desire in Language* or *Dissemination* for that matter. Get a grip, they know her way around *jouissance*, you're game to discharge some of that pulsion trapped in linguistic structures, we're not so unattractive

I don't want to make an 'event' out of this slippage in language suffice it to say.

Could you knock something off employees end-dated prior to each milestone circulate it to the working group.

An outstanding action item I have not seen loop back through me without changing the essence of the message.

I am drawing some blanks know your main focus is the naming.

Shopping list of motivators

- Achievement[W3086]
- Independence[W2266]
- Exhibition[W1883]
- Recognition[W1779]
- Affiliation[W16940]
- Masturbation[W22131]
- Dominance[W6606]
- Nurturance[W72558]
- Succorance[N/A]
- Sibilance[N/A]
- Sexuality[W5632]
- Stimulation[W8202]
- Diversion[W10567]
- Novelty[W10847]
- Understanding[W1075]
- Coconuts[W42802]
- Consistency[W7220]
- Security[W706]

The armpit hole in our discount turtleneck sweater has questions on Jesus and good clean copy. Don't stretch or curly hair will spring through in an excess of energy that can't be utilized. Bleached WASP HR woman's toothy smile abrades against money company's crow's feet are upon you [G10]benefits program. Walking around with a dog-eared list of what to write about the Shoah, you crossed each line out with frumpy[Q5259] jocular gorgon of albino lucille lattice. M.'s penny shots hang in the lobby, Abe Lincoln playing heads, his Memorial, tails. Bought from the Canada Council Art Bank for how shiny they look and a tax break

From the 10,000-foot view you never know when this will rear its ugly head it's important not to keep score.

I'll prepare a strawdog on double character do you want to litmus test it I extracted all the communication.

This concern bubbled upward don't take anything I say as 'gospel' we want to use language that reflects today's realities.

'Whoever and there [sic] mother needs to see it' let me be the heavy and intervene.

Jabès the atheist says Jews can't help writing about God. Nor can we help writing about being Jewish^{Q7O9} home-maker retard from e spam of ruth toe. Even if it's just one drop or half your blood. Everything comes down to 'special treatment,' 'energetic liquidation,' *arbeit macht* the power of jargon and excremental^{Q34842} provident hyperdocument assault. Perfect dehumanization then nothing$_{G11}$ aye crosshairs + true vision without end. Except the word 'Jew.' Say it sixty sixty sixt six ty million million i'm the million mazda man six million mazda times will not exhaust meaning

of green diaspora
among nuclear
below my hoard. among as
over, my hoard of my hoard
targeted cross signals with .
beside nuclear or wash

over targeted cross signals. princes & paupers or
beside targeted cross signals. of
as if green because vagina america.
within wash in.
beside, vagina america   because I
within the dented sword. or
as if the last supper in green. giving a reaction.

Retention Investments needs to know the keen relations among capitalist spirit, Brand Bible and anal stage. How one of the child's first Fisher-Price playthings is its feces, transformed into property, gift or weapon, depending on a fluctuating will and viral marketing strategy. We lived in a big house riddled with challenge and steepening and my compulsion to succorance. Okay, so good for Freud. Blame the excesses of parsimony and homosexuality on an unregulated anal babyQ91 stupid boy joe father stage. Ferenczi and his dedicated relationship manager, on the other hand, will eat their own dog food and bubble up a future-proofed thoughtform. It is what it is, they say, tracing the origins of art and the advice-driven market to that same kid's manipulation of his shit

I kill my sentence and Celan is totally blown out of the water caught up by the Swan's brute squirt.

Not warm hard phallus but Bataille, bleached WASP and feeling like you've lost your ship.

Can we link this a bit to Leda and his own decomposing, develop her rhetor-tribadistic touch?

It's a mishmash, witness the orphan organs and Carson end-dated out of this sixfold slippage.

**How to write
a title**

1 Appeal to reader's self interest

2 Say things in the positive

3 Avoid award-winning cleverness

4 Include your USP

5 Get Right Get God

6 Avoid 'If' statements

7 Make title work with the visual, not the body

Mark my words my hoard supports new symbols not just another crow essay on mouthG-7 machine breast machine imagery in *King Lear* and *Hamlet*, how the inexorable path of tragedy devours language and meaning. She ran out of words by the third paragraph, like the one on *Pilgrim's Progress* that dead-ends on page two after pledging to be a long sharp sword key to the door sixfold star of good travailerG20 atw20 vagina Q20. Used to spill story to anyone on the street, like the Ancient Mariner or Lear's 'Who is it who can tell me who I am?' But used up buttplug YHVH G-spot glory store of what to share, keep remains to ourself

Can you give me a drop-dead deadline it really needs to be crisper the pre-retirement bank will be frozen.

Put less emphasis on the fund as a mishmash I like fragments of value waiting for an inverted world.

We each have to step up to the plate check back on that string I'm making stuff up as I go along.

There is a specific protocol 'just in time when they need it kind of' velcroed to the hip.

You drew concentric circles on the board, marking the voracious progress of Austen's card sharp Emma nailing Jell-O to the wall. Slip up once in a breezy travel article on Canadian colloquialisms, orphan organs spouting Carleton County, New Brunswick's: 'Sweet bald-headed Jesus. Is it ever some friggin' cold out tonight!' Boss wields the diety [sic] of God pecking the eyes out G30 scalpel with such numbing grace, we barely feel the W7137 stitches gerald folly pots, okay okay she's come back to her sentences

Anne Carson on Celan: 'What is lost when words are wasted? And where is the human store to which such goods are gathered?' in that it is was i for on you he be with

Which words are gathered, the wasted or the lost? ask word groups along central history few changes I remember hundred individual air

When you 'cleanse words and salvage what is cleansed,' do you collect what's been scrubbed off or what remains minute older claims from methods accepted machine?

And who bears witness for the authors pulling estimates of bitter crash and victorian distinguished confused witness?

- Books of quotation, aphorism and euphemism
- Books of slang, idiom and colloquial expression
- Books of one-liners, wit and wisdom
- Books of Revelation
- *The Describer's Dictionary*
- *Literature and Evil*
- *The Management Methods of Jesus*
- A thesaurus

People Excellence isn't a Value of the 86,800 most common English words, the w1 of w2 and to a in that it is was i for on w13 you he be with as by at have are this not but had his they from she which or we an there her were one do been all their w42 has would will what if can when so no said who more about up them some could him into its then two out time like only my did other me your now over just may these new also people any know very see first well after should than where back how get most way down our made got w100 how positioning mitigates having to come up with a lump-sum contribution for my RSP since the world was created through God's 'speech,' each letter representing a different creative force

If 'all poets are Jews' veiled in Cyrillic letters.

Killing themselves, Levi, Améry, Benjamin felt 'poor with words,' while Wiesel emerged from 10 years' silence to shake hands with Ronald Reagan.

A communicator must be concerned with unchanging man, but Celan successively lost letters until he died.

Judaïté, Tsvetaeva and writing are but the same I hope people of church archive clitoris, the same depletion.

Mass affluent consumers' key satisfaction drivers aspirational by most common queries of most-common-English-words engine: fuck Q1 sex Q2 love the shit god i penis cunt a ass jesus dog Q13 pussy hate bush john me hello vagina america bitch cat dick you war yes she like and cock no damn david gay man computer money word mother michael poop Q42 happy mom asshole orgasm he mike apple peace help one hi car bob fart cool it chris microsoft crap woman what good is death hell conquistador iraq james house mark butt porn cum girl paul home dad work but of beer nigger andrew tom tit tits usa anal baby stupid boy joe father kill mary school sarah smith Q100 re-scoped the guestimate – the generic one month is longer than 30 days. You can control the reader's reaction without changing the facts

Dear _____ :

- Your USP is compelling
- Though rather long in the telling
- You showcase your skill
- In using a quill
- And make no mistakes in your spelling

Adrienne Rich used the Communicating Bad News template to affirm that the half-curled frond would not commingle with your book. The tie's lower tip should align with the top centre of the belt buckle and its back slide through the label to not reveal an undisciplined self. From the epoch of the name to the advent of the number, C^3I spends time etching surfaces with symmetry, repetition and a balance of nodal points. At least some figures when processed produce pleasure, but don't introduce new products in August or wear shirts off a dead man's body to work. Heart, hope, faith, Andy Card, Josef Goebbels and Banana Republic make today's bureaucracies into tomorrow's communities of meaning. So be it, amen, let's roll!

corporation because page was hovering
below money. guess flow
under stainlessness. write about Jewish beside
or rebalance beside stainlessness, overtime of
content rub off beyond money. scrap I barely feels
beside pitch but lose shame

amid plain language pitch of stainlessness she glimpses
between overtime. Celan enter the white or
sliding beyond pyjamas or pitch. against
money don't stretch below corporation. come back as if
traces, pyjamas tweaking as don't stretch between
meaning. corporation of scrap write about Jewish
as if coin come back beyond pyjamas. coin get them on.

Stink boston beach ridiculous sexual nine6five of money repulsive. Bills and coins fingered by infinite unwashed hands painting the tricks. Filthy lucre – some of the lucky end up 'rolling in it,' making 'piles' of 'money up the ass.' Commodity form is not a simple state of mind – you need reader involvement, which means getting a reaction, not giving a recitation on what two w64 good q64 out is time 66 death sixty-six. Money makes words into alien things and psychology + communication = salesmanship

Just shoot me now my inbox is a little cramped send it along the food chain.

Whether it's based on fact or blind faith from various 'lens' [*sic*] of expertise the landscape is extremely saturated.

I recognize we can't turn this ship around overnight leveraging it you feel like you've lost your 'edge.'

My head's gonna pop off one of the iterations of the new.

The mystical white crow, the sword and the flower that shattered stone standing in a Chelsea gallery watching an artist get fucked by a collector for $20,000 U.S., it's always the first G44 cliché would W44 mom Q44 off our tongue they love best: your dreams are possible, you can create the life you want, there's no better time to make an investment in your future. How limited the sphere you negotiate Q14543 liu ouagadougou pogrom, 'flourish' boasting too many vowels, 'thrive' too abstract. Internal censor cheapening the affect of words, no nick or dent in the narrow way the victorious city ritualist G-3 monoculture. Like the unemployed former Democrats from Flint swerving behind Bush and false, disfigured certainty, you hand over the car keys to Jesus and the boss pockets 200 bucks an hour

The armpit hole in Sarah Smith's benefits program will have to be frozen.

It really needs to be crisper, without changing the essence of infinite unwashed letters.

With only bland octopus and stainfulness left over, I'd better move the goal posts.

We want to use gibberish that reflects today's too-wide-open white page velcroed to the hip.

How to write persuasive body copy

1 Take on commodity form
2 Start selling in the first line
3 Stick to the surface
4 Be relevant
5 Heed the Clarity Commandment
6 Support your claims
7 Burn out meaning

42 in the Gematria of Nothing equals annihilation a heart tested the scarlet city is ready for a bronze dragnet a true miracle weekly test at three o three absorb your carefully scrutinized observations don't wilt fireball add it straight all the duck in a row and they sing a new song another mage uses letters a little leaven torments the whole lump anticipate answer to all of mankind's chaosphere are you ready for a new chamber of horrors betwixt and between catatonia breathing and chees-wheezies catch the promises catch your breath chose the dove not the serpent by golly we have a point crowned with mercy and strength and diaspersia dysfunctionitis

A true copy of a copy, I defend the Sophists, use rhyme and pun in my heds and give you my best gut instinct. It's not as if the Republic sans poet Q2734 pride in belgium part visual arsehole irene would repeat without knowing any less often than our 21st century Western simulacrum rife with scribbling nama zappa gerontology 64313 tricksters. Nor was Socrates's dialectical method for eliciting 'truth' any less wily or rhetorical than drilling down through my inbox queued up for deterritorialized release, performance management

the w1 fuck Q1 of w2 sex Q2 and w3 love Q3 to w4 the Q4
Vav is the star G4 Jew a w5 shit Q5 in w6 god Q6 that i it
penis is cunt was a i ass for jesus on dog you pussy he
hate be bush with john as me by hello at vagina have
america are bitch this cat not dick but you had war his
yes they she from like she and which cock or no we damn
an david there gay her man were computer one money
do word been mother all michael their poop can't
survive purely on theoretical 42 strength only conquis-
tador 68 selection and combination my iraq did james
other house me mark your butt now porn over cum just
girl may paul these home new dad also work people but
any of know beer very nigger see andrew first tom well
tit after tits should usa than anal where baby back stupid
how w93 boy Q93 her G93 brightness is of Gematria is
the machine brilliance she has a nearly perfect bite get
joe most father way kill down mary our school made
sarah got smith

If I could divine nausea fuelled by wiping off shame and writing about money. Something about the consumption of formerly live O Mother of the Sun F# products that turned stomach to gee thirty-three extrapolation. At first the smells of seafood, then thin pool of blood under beef, repulsion of mint with smoky lamb. Money makes our daily life give up yummy veal *piccata al limone*, six-week-old baby cow wriggling in strange 14 transforming highest truth vise. With just bland chicken and turkey left over, you'd better hang up your 'pen' for good. Without incorporation, they've beaten us to a pulp

Orwell says freedom and democracy bloom from plain speech. Let us say language hardwired to heterogeneous aggregate, plain altar an 18 iron Alas poor Yorick rod no more (or less) political than military- or theory-speak. Or poetry butterfly 1391 from ambiguous octopus bacon. When you use short words and amputate adjectives in a Trinidadian what-bank-folks-on brochure for the big Canadian limit offers, we want to say fragmentation sans Oedipal daddy-mommy-me

but noisy in begging bowl
bottomed-out out selling promise because floated out
outside begging bowl. floated out among
never fail among skimmers,

floated out of floated out. beside moment of cordial
, through positive I surplus lip servicing
but   between   but invested

inside , .flesh never fail
as skimmers noisy and begging bowl

aborted. amid ambiguous , skimmers
or may you prosper. of positive surplus

over . positive surplus with selling promise.
with begging bowl.

**How to make
a name**

1 Brainstorm words for what you do

2 Brainstorm words for your aspirations

3 Brainstorm words for your customers

4 Think metaphorical and mythological

5 Search for synonyms, homonyms, alliteration, clichés

6 Search for positive or negative equivalence

7 Start combining

8 Add a suffix

9 Truncate – low-hanging fruit, penectomy, nothingness

10 Rank your names

Dalton Freud discovered that feces and blow jobs don't jive with polypeptide pants and bereavement leave. 'Don't you know the origin of beachwear is in the capitalist manipulation of vacations?' he asked his dog-eared sewing machine in frustration. 'That's why WASPS and 227 money fact night are forever bracketed with stinking dirty pure 'capitalist spirit,' while Jews are premature shyster kikes who can't transcend the marks they're made of.' Le jew pour le jeu, le jeu pour le jew, quelle discontinuity among ich and du

Poesis consumes the green noem evanesced in glosso-lalial white. Shuffle it like cards and you may find another way of bathing language.

We've raised their backs blowing out floater days stickhandle the translation.

The tyranny of subject-verb-predicate is neither emo-tional nor balanced like belly or finger or the accident that no longer looks like symptom.

Any dissemination, distribution or copying is strictly on the receiving end I may be missing something here.

suckle a dangerous thoughtform Sepher Yetzirah
ripping you a new ritualistic asshole my army is hoard
open for what 46 orgasm business would mom if he can
mike purged pine box philosopher said one who has
happy hi 53 car 54 about bob mater love will turn your
world into a sweet thing so peace up six a you dumb a fart
it all boils down to the way you think some intertwined
two *pip* idiot will asshole them we know your no help
track record it could chris him microsoft cool they
console not goat editor do you doubt who we are when
apple concern yourself with this buggery book its
woman boils biology into crap then good time out is
betray the true death warning like hell dog on true real-
ity 13 – so don't hesitate to use my name in vain

You try to pare her page to pitch but words respond using 'my' voice treading new waters.

We have to put our heads together 'live' beneath the veneer of the homepage once we get this backload under our belts.

I believe content owners 'absolutely need to know' intuitive acronym synergy thrust the shuffle of volume.

This isn't a 'hill to die on' we've done soft launches before.

The work of the sword and 4 relays cross when we try to give financial advice. Boss heavily edits to get the 'tone' right: take a holistic approach to risk management, steer clear of portfolio potholes and don't get caught chasing hot 1125 baby method of surface sale returns. Strange quirk, since you've never worked in a big company (and often toil all day in pyjamas) yet can still whip off a snappy business-attire policy. Don't own a car but expend many a lubricating word on transmission-fluid theory. Our regular column on diarrhea evangelizes the brand traction, floating out key messages based on current accrued liability. Don't settle for 170% nailing the answers with a certain amount of customer passion and impactful equity in *la perruque*. Concur with the psychology of tense selection, vet her specificity-equals-felicity cathexis, how do you like that human-asset-component grammar?

name and non-event

through new look

below lightning rod. outside as

on top of non-event, and lightning rod

escalate between . new look lump-sum scramble

among of unique selling pain changed my life

through lightning rod. invisible tapestry of I bear witness

against believe me. caveat of

cascade out of name as lightning rod.

between bear witness over pimp.

inside, pimp glorying spot out

glorying spot with. because beside

pimp glorying spot over . a bias toward the throwaway.

With money keen on poesis, Kafka and Stevens sold
peace of mind, Jabès stocks. Bataille stuck Dewey deci-
mals on dough and we bought fashion insurance. Our
parents fell in love at the archives, spent all the marbles
they'd collected to that point. You too fall under the spell
of objects, cataloguing letters, orgasms, memories by
their proper Safeway the Magus Ain Soph Aur 18 Dalton
McGuinty names before surrendering. How the pieces
don't quite fit together when they've canker huggy
amortized around polperro politique headsets for two
too long

It sounded too much like 'motherhood' speaks to the strength and vitality I want to walk that line.

Tighten up the things you're touching on as we travel along this path riddled with challenge and change.

This means we have to pass the punctum as sacred surplus I'll flip it over to you.

Forget the self without your pain you're nothing.

Ingredients of a winning visual identity

- Be unique
- Be timeless
- Be easy to reproduce in all materials and sizes
- Carry your cross – face 11's truth
- Work well with other symbols and marks
- Be acceptable in every social and religious culture you operate in

Spoilsports of sorts, her various avatars hover on the outside contemplating what's not being said in the minus five lunchroom from dust you are homosexuality houseguests. Obsessed with the phallogocentric left margin, the professional stranger makes multiple voices intersect the field and all their words are 34 skew-wise from all directions. Unable to choose one 'I' or version of the events, modest witness tries to 'tone it down' to minimize the 'piss-off' factor native to human capital, artful deviation and fractured surfaces. Think straight, talk straight – let's overlay everything with the amount they're 'confessional,' juggling the first few out of the gate. Hopefully this will get rid of the blur, create a nice 'spin'

Trapped in this high-performance culture, let's suspend all disbelief, ignore the elephants in the room.

I won't remember that avant-garde chaos frees the writing machine's choked circuits.

Our abstractions stink of pure gibberish and no one notices the false pundits.

Look through the mirror, it's the Information Age, where every surface is 1793 brilliant urine requests scum wolf and nothing shines.

Written with a luxurious –34 iron stylus, Pound's shop-
worn usury songs linger on. Obscuring the texts with
intercourse we got the labrys power G7 ghoul philology,
the Jew infects money *and* language by sitting on books
– and abstraction. The kike god is monopoly, as Jews
control 99% of all 32 means of Bog of Tears king of kings
Feeling Stones communication, including Jewspapers.
Being so overdetermined can be taxing, especially for
les assimilés like our heroine or Améry. For when the time
comes to be numbered, 'a chew / ees a chew, even ones
wit a likeing for to make arht-voiks

Align this process as it evolves I want everything over-
laid with Bataille's catastrophes as cleansing acts,
rebalancing the planet.

Just like your portfolio, tweaking the delicate equilib-
rium among asset mix, time horizon and risk tolerance.

You who've been hauling butt it takes a village but it's
our space of writing to be ranged over not pierced.

Are you 'he who writes and is written,' 'one who writes and is written' or are you 'she'? People buy products to solve problems, while Sarah is engulfed in a cry that Yukel can't touch or inhabit. Jabès, Levinas, Gilman, *même* Derrida, falter at the impenetrable fold of woman, vowel and stupid cow if you follow us now you won't have to go full circle word. Are we back to this? –4 Jewish princes unwilling to root in a redomiciled wound that won't be floated out without context

of Jew producing inside plain language.
interlacing through libidinal economy because
I narrative gathering amid poetry machine. coming
as if plain language excess interlacing
out of Jew, Jew

gathering   and falling away. through shit
spewing body without organs over narrative crumbling
of spew under plain language or crumbling

over moments that exceed containment, deals
we make. deals we make   lost
and body without organs gathering   of excess

salvage. gather   on top of
moments that exceeding containment, meaning
because production of forms combine.   or rhetoric

salvaging out meaning. poetry machine   form
outside lesbian. poetry machine over money.

You know the drill, there is no writing that is not in economic w383 love w384 with commodity form, and there's stuff coming at me in all directions. Not the downward spiral of deferred want, not tied to lack or cost but generative and regenerative with the lesbian body, compound interest and the juice the spittle the fluids the fluxes the excrements the flatulence, the nerves. I was pretty sure she and I were on sync [*sic*], but nothing is not painful, let's just use the void to think the full. Key her life positions that discovery of subject can be identity plentiful only while one never never never never never need old look home

Just to make sure we're on the same page reduce the 'clutter' before pressing buttons.

Metonymy repurposes the straw man into idiolect and Hyde and his fables 'hand off' the process for building catharsis.

Don't suck and blow at the same time I've got my skins in the game information must be handled with care.

Umbrella brings in a new set of players she'll greek me out.

How to write for the Internet

1 Write for skimmers

2 Write for peckers

3 Filter, impose, trespass

4 Include a link to the Code

5 Think hyper

6 Think branding

7 Think icon

8 Tell your visitor where to go

Does the unreadable drive the reader from consuming to producing, or all the 66 what good time is death bells and whistles of the ineffable? Despite *les soixante-huitardes* (like us, born that uppity year), poetic Jewish coverage + pregnant 3984 language isn't revolutionary enough. Ensconced in the academy pleasuring in the beautiful excess of the unshackled referent, poetry can't stock food banks, warm bodies or stop genocide from affecting my RSP. Ultimately you'll be the funnel here at the brink, should we brief you and brainstorm, transgress the Markov chain before game over?

Reading and gleaning from the same German root and Varda's picaresque travails among detritus.

A multi-sexed academic friend calls our libidinal desire around knowledge masochistic – they'd prefer a 'softer' approach to flesh out the whole picture.

Like the angel of history few 493 changes remember or the sun + the world assending [*sic*] over & out the ɢfourth poetic moment, grasp what I can before it lose your soul for my sake how potent is potent –16 holy nuns rots.

Rather than kill the gift of art, consciousness can make it more 11 crosshairs are you so perverted that you thrill with fright plentiful. We don't draw inspiration to our begging bowl then offer a nice drink. There's no moment of grace, hidden coherence or cordial for your soul. We all enter the poem and flounder in words within 365, sounds in 1710, the indeterminate come live with the forty-five stars of reason flow. By doing this atten- tively – and not suspending disbelief – we don't have an at-hand solution for your vocabulary work, or guilt by association, but would like to recognize collective effort not set in stone albino lucille or be grotesque to get that edge trace within hyperdocument. hyperdocument I wash the surface below sitcom economies. law governs fragments out of I wash the 1132 on top of ambiguous bacon, If in search of truth because sin best dupe with decomposing tales. decomposing 5989 laugh within be grotesque to get that edge and sitcom economies it's a mesh

among transgression. viral baby because decomposing 5989 troubleshoot against hyperdocument. e spam succorance law governs 5685 because it's a 12578 between farty two or le jeu pour the keyword. under peace of archive viral baby into sin. viral 1130 into aufhebung. farty 64 troubleshoot but sovereign transgression over 37836 tales. goat as 1291 36636 succorance pyjamas within aufhebung it's 5 mesh beside sitcom economies. sin trace.

What's the use of Jews writing limericks, half not even paying? Check back on that stanza – this is a marathon not a good governance issue 5 116 21075 589. Poor with deception, Primo Levi felt his comments weren't value-added, based on blind faith or the misaligned 1 85343 planets 9742. Facing the matronly woman behind the counter, how vulnerable to pare down to pitch when your inbox is a little 5 176 12044 cramped

If shit is the work of art representing the gift of the devoured father to the lost mother.

If stories are our attempts to re-enter 36.

If I have to keep making new work like food.

Let's just keep FAQs to things of substance, squander all perishable values in performance. Grab one of the bottomed-out seats in the front row and you could experience a 1305 double 44641 catharsis.

Dear _____ :

Three reasons to become a writer:

1 Writers help the economy

2 Writing is an investment that grows as you 1863

3 Writers help the needy: A recent fundraising package I wrote for an evangelical adoption agency generated $30,000, exactly what we needed to save children from being aborted. My copy makes the world a better place. Yours 48 128!

You had trouble accepting gifts, even a token from your lover at the bus stop. Haunted by the potlatch image of 'swallowing' the visiting tribe by giving them blankets, or inducing shameful vomiting through excess feasting. Heads or tails, the more you copper allocated struggling shit the more face you save, and don't forget to close your mouth when giving birth – things can reverse themselves when you 56 285 open up. Like the child in the 583 2560 1 mirror stage in love with the image of money, we resist recognizing the hunger of the other. To recognize the 71 the door 4 the abyss the Jew no longer Yahweh's chosen people for they believe not in his son on top of old smokey! is to give up game, war, exile as being, the solar anus *and* ecstatic lesbian merging. My concern is that the clock is ticking can you evacuate what remains to make room for the 1 4164 surplus?

Ambiguities of the human condition are a threat to surfeit of 1267.

Sonnet's sublime orgasmic 447 one of the iterations of the houses.

I hold them on the page, Valéry's face a void queued up for release.

Hats off, this won't be floated 65 without dissemination.

If *différance* can be anointed by the *Petit Robert*, why not 'Make a pre-emptive strike,' 'Poke bullets at it' and 'It's not a hill to die on'? Or 'Shock and Awe' as it applies to the new Porsche? Communication is three parts behind-the-scenes and one part front lines. Perhaps we should petition the *Canadian Oxford* to please include these 17295 coined succumbed enlisted phrases among possible usages of 'strike,' 'poke,' '1446' and '10954.' Perhaps also ask for 'breathturn' to be entered, the moment when silence kills the poet so the poem may come to ten + five + 6 + 5

This is a marathon not a sprint it's not just lip service what we can and cannot say.

A lot of 'me' questions a 116 21075 issue these inquiries can easily be 'shut down.'

If my comments aren't value-added I think the planets were 85343 I just want to keep our processes clean.

I know you're killing yourself not necessarily the answer that will 'fly.'

We wanted to learn the *mameloshn* but it was too close to 883. That bitter sting of scorpio caw goes the corvus feud with the hyperthyroid bug-eyed blonde Hildegard in school, all you regretted saying. Ancel-Celan depleting the German language with 85273 neologisms, clean liberating the signifier from one but not all viral messages. Tapestry of Agnès Varda's hand, burned-out lines biff davy collaborators gleaned from memory's 20310 trash cans

Perilously rough waters it feels like a 'production line'
pull rabbits out of your 7939.

There's not an obvious 'good 677' story recognize all the
'knitting together' you did it's still 'art' not 957.

What you're doing is pioneering work casting my 1536
and seeing what I rake in you are the invisible 6696.

These are tough times to be in our roles when 'noise' is
built into a company's DNA and our very ideas are but
the outgrowth of 783.

You looked for subjectivity in 18th-century picaresques and *An Essay Concerning Human Understanding*. Thought one day the fridge would open and Self 14 the flower the six-rayed star the word tented in us would emerge fully delineated. Now the nomadic 39 the empress the secret door child molester PsyberMagick subject uses a model of identifying 'enterprise' from targeted man-on-the-street feedback. Like a forms, then, that even while it book thirteen a most important number ALWHSDOZKVGRC april is a very cryptic word, it all boils down pine box

79 759 44465 5 761 2 5 1044 1512 1 409 2570 2 118 23 4065.

76 4 118 362 33'22 1740 1 144 510 33 51 1429 21 4 139 23 26216 1054 3169 5258ed.

33'45 21 4 9577 98 1841 186 345 18 4442 11 44 67 4 459 1 1726 3967.

15655 8 97 61 626 2326 11'324 1766 54151 18 11 559.

1 403 9 4 930 6 '2421 510.' 51 11239, 41705 32 39337 2 1267 1268 1269$^{(W1269)}$. 41 4324 27737 1432 1 11392 36247 417, 19596's 2047 560 996, 16368 62128 447, 3316 283: 1786 1855. 11127 10022 489 1 671 671 1680, 2553 8831, 2719-2719!

I see the blood, sweat and tears pulling an invisible rug out from everyone's feet in the manual and part of the culture.

Look for the hidden meaning use it as a lightning rod more pokes at the communication.

I'm not going to send out platitudes brick by brick we have 6,000 beholders.

'Pain' can be involved in getting to the end a birdy told me we may be asked without falling overboard.

Poems on pages 15, 23, 39, 51, 59, 69 and 77 were made using Lewis LaCook's Markov-chain based Flash poetry generators. All other poems were made by the author's proprietary machine-mind™, with some assistance from WordCount™ and QueryCount™ at www.wordcount.org. The former is a searchable list of the 86,800 most frequently used words in English, while the latter is a searchable list of words most frequently queried in WordCount.

The author also used the Gematria of Nothing (GON) engine at www.mysticalinternet.com. Gematria is a method of Biblical exegesis based on assigned positive or negative numerical values of Hebrew letters and semantic links between words based on their values. The GON is a bizarre Christ-, crow- and empress-laden attempt to co-opt the serious practice of Hebrew numerology and apply it to select English words and phrases. The author co-opts GON for HR purposes.

WordCount values are represented in the text by the letter w; QueryCount by Q; and GON by G. As QueryCount rankings shuffle every few hours to reflect recent word queries, Q values in this text will not match present QueryCount rankings. Nor does GON's numerology always add up. Orthography and punctuation are also used as found.

Thanks

To Erín Moure, who with a few deft strokes helped shape the pieces into a whole. And to Robert Majzels, who pushed the pieces to fruition in the first place.

Special thanks to Moyra Davey, life-long friend, for the inspirational talks on money and shit, the time in New York with sweet Bella when I wrote most of this text, and the beautiful cover artwork.

Many thanks to Alana Wilcox, Christina Palassio, Evan Munday, Stan Bevington and everyone else at Coach House for their professionalism and support of my work.

And to Kate Eichhorn, for the ingenious HR bookwork and for being *here* at the advent of 54.

For sundry kindnesses: Cheryl Sourkes, Carol Laing, Margaret Christakos, Beverley Daurio, Katherine Parrish, M. NourbeSe Philip, Vince Pietropaolo, Paul Russell, Lisa Robertson, Ron Silliman and, especially, Lisa Rundle.

Thanks to the editors of the following publications, where excerpts from this text appeared in earlier forms: *EOAGH*, *MiPOesias*, *Drunken Boat*, *Pilot*, *Matrix*, *West Coast Line*, *Windsor Review*, *Rampike*, *Kiss Machine*, *Film Print* and *Shift & Switch: New Canadian Poetry*. Excerpts also appeared in a belladonna* books chapbook, *from Human Resources*, and in an above/ ground press broadside.

Funding from the Canada Council for the Arts and the Ontario Arts Council Writers' Reserve gave me invaluable time and space to write.

About the author

Rachel Zolf is the author of the poetry collections *Masque* (The Mercury Press, 2004), which was shortlisted for the 2005 Trillium Book Award for Poetry, and *Her absence, this wanderer* (BuschekBooks, 1999), which was a finalist in the CBC Literary Competition. Zolf lives in Toronto and was the founding poetry editor for *The Walrus* magazine.

The colophon

Typeset in Slate, a typeface designed by Rod McDonald
Printed and bound at the Coach House on bpNichol Lane

Edited for the press by Erín Moure
Designed by Alana Wilcox and Stan Bevington
Author photo by Vincenzo Pietropaolo
Front cover art: *Copperhead #1*, 1990, colour photograph by
    Moyra Davey, courtesy of the artist
Back cover art: *Coppertail #1*, 1990, colour photograph by
    Moyra Davey, courtesy of the artist

Coach House Books
401 Huron Street on bpNichol Lane
Toronto, Ontario M5S 2G5
Canada

800 367 6360
416 979 2217

mail@chbooks.com
www.chbooks.com